PROVE IT ALL NIGHT!

The BRUCE SPRINGSTEEN Trivia Book

Deborah Mayer

Mustang Publishing
New Haven

For Mark
because this book would not exist without him.

And for Bruce
because this book would not exist without him, either!

Copyright © 1987 by Deborah Mayer.

All rights reserved. No portion of this book may be repro-
duced in any form without the permission of the publisher.
Published in the United States of America by Mustang
Publishing Company, Inc., P.O. Box 9327, New Haven, Con-
necticut, 06533. Manufactured, printed, and, of course, born
in the U.S.A.

Distributed to the trade by Kampmann and Co., New York.

Library of Congress Cataloging in Publication Data:
Mayer, Deborah, 1960-
   Prove it all night!

   1. Springsteen, Bruce.   2. Rock musicians--United
States--Miscellanea.   I. Title.
ML420.S77M38   1987   784.5′4′00924   87-1569
ISBN 0-914457-17-9

10 9 8 7 6 5 4 3 2 1

Acknowledgements

Countless people contributed encouragement and suggestions to this book. So, a big thank you to the following:

To my family—Sandra, Howard, David, and Stuart Mayer—for putting up with me, and Sarah Williams and Frances Cowan for always being there.

To Diana Geffner, Jane Brody, Cathy Geier, and Jean Altieri Coscia—my roommates past and present—for having enough patience to live with someone whose musical taste rarely strays outside the state of New Jersey.

To Cindy Berg, Annie Brenenson, Jason Brabazon, Cindy Compitello, Charles Cross and *Backstreets*, Marty Crouse, Dalton Delan, John Fielding and Barbara Vagliano, "The Faithful," Danielle Frizzi, Mary Jo Fiorentino, the staff of Imero Fiorentino Associates (especially Tony Salerno, Donna Roseman, and Larry Sedwick), Carol Gerber and family, Bobby Giambone, Phyllis Hayes, Alice Herb, Donna and Doreen Hughes, Lisa Iannucci, Maureen Kueny, Michelle Leone, Phil Lewis, Linda Mastropaolo, Michael McCarthy, Lee Mrowicki and the Pony, Dulcie Neiman, Bert Padell, Debbie Elbin Penchina, Janine Pietrucha, Leela Pitenis, Jim Ryan, Arlen Schumer, Matty Stragazzi, Mark Tatelman, Maureen Vanterpool, Diane Wilkinson, The Asbury Park Rock 'n Roll Museum (Stephen Bumball and Billy Smith), and the staff of *ABC News Closeup* for their advice, encouragement, and for not bumping me off the word processor.

Very special thanks to Nancy Barr, John Corio, David Denenberg, Rollin Riggs, Debra Rothenberg, Doron and Ori Scharf, Robert Urband, Kathi Van Zandt, and Steve Zuckerman.

And most of all, thanks to Mark Ashkinos for everything.

Contents

Introduction

A few months ago, during a slow night at a New York club called Heartbreak, my friend Mark suggested we play "Bruce trivia." Whoever got three questions wrong had to buy the next round of drinks. Mark bought me a lot of drinks that night. He also suggested that I write a book. At first I laughed, but a week later I was locked in the library and glued to the word processor. I had a great time researching and writing this book, and I hope you don't feel frustrated if you can't answer a lot of the questions. Some of them are so obscure, I doubt even Bruce could answer them!

I was twelve years old when *Greetings from Asbury Park, N.J.* was released in January, 1973. I wasn't terribly impressed. But by September, when *The Wild, the Innocent and the E Street Shuffle* appeared, Bruce was Number One in my heart. I played Side 2 so often that I had to replace my original copy (and I've replaced it yet again). Bruce took chances with his music at a stage in his career when he really couldn't afford to be too risky. Who else would dare to release an album with just three songs on one side—two beautiful ballads with a joyful rocker in between?

I entered high school when *Born to Run* came out, and every morning, as I got dressed for school, WNEW-FM played the day's "Bruce Juice." If I overslept and missed it, my day was ruined. Bruce's music had become even more adventurous, and, in the height of the disco craze, listening to "Thunder Road" and "Backstreets" was like breathing fresh air.

In college, my friends and I took road trips around the New York area, catching as many shows on the "Darkness" tour as we could. Those remain my favorite shows. Bruce was wild, unpredictable, and great fun; you never knew what he'd play or what he'd do on stage. Tickets were easy to get, and each show was unique.

Years later, I spent warm summer nights outside Tower Records, waiting for tickets to one of Bruce's stadium shows. I was once lucky enough to be 15th in line, and I spent nearly 24 hours surrounded by teenage boys who were being paid by scalpers to wait for tickets. But the six shows I saw at Giants Stadium were disappointing. The music was still incredible, but the shows seemed much too staged and predictable. And, worst of all, Bruce didn't play "Rosalita," although the crowd screamed for it all night. I left feeling that Bruce concerts—at least for long-time Bruce fans—might be better left to our memories.

But writing this book helped me remember why I love Bruce's music so much. The research helped soothe the disappointment I felt from the stadium shows. The Bruce I loved has changed—he's no longer a cult figure and I'm no longer the only girl on the block who isn't scared by the grubby, bearded face on the cover of *Born to Run*. Bruce is now a superstar, and he must meet that demand, even though my friends and I still fantasize that we'll hear him play "Incident on 57th Street" some night at the Bottom Line.

I still love a great rock 'n roll road trip, only now I often see another New Jersey musician, John Eddie, whose spirit matches Bruce's in the old days. But there's still only one Bruce Springsteen, and for better or worse, I will always love his music more than anyone's.

Deborah Mayer
December, 1986

The Questions

At least he learned something in Catholic school.
(photo: Nancy Barr)

Q and A #1

Growin' Up

1. What was the name of the Catholic grade school Bruce attended?

2. What was the name of the first band he played with?

3. Who was Bruce's first writing partner?

4. Where did Bruce first record?

5. Name one of the two songs he recorded there.

6. How much did the recording time cost?

7. What broke during the recording session?

8. Name three of the six members of Bruce's first band.

9. When Bruce was growing up, he lived in a house next to a gas station. Who ran that station?

10. What college did Bruce attend briefly?

11. What did Bruce have published while in college?

12. Bruce has two sisters. Name one of them.

13. What is the maiden name of Bruce's mother?

14. What did she do for work?

15. When Bruce was a boy, he saw a performer on TV who inspired him to play the guitar. Who was it?

Home of the famous
"shuffle" and "freeze-out"
(photo: Deborah Mayer)

16. Where are 10th Avenue and E Street?

17. Who lived there?

18. Where can you find Madame Marie?

19. In 1968, Bruce began hanging out at an Asbury Park club called the Upstage. Who ran this club?

20. Who taught Bruce how to drive?

21. When Bruce got a guitar at age 13, where was it purchased?

22. How much did the guitar cost?

23. Who taught him his first chords?

24. Why did the manager of his first band have the time to manage the band?

25. How much money did their manager make other than his percentage from the band's income?

26. Where was the band's first gig?

27. How much did they get paid?

28. What song did they close with?

29. How did Bruce and George Theiss meet?

30. What was Bruce told after he first auditioned for the band?

(Answers on page 66.)

Bonus Question #1

Though cars and driving figure prominently in Bruce's lyrics, he sings about only two gas stations. Name them.

Answer: Exxon and Texaco

Match-Up Quiz #1

— On The Backstreets —

Match the song to the album on which it appears:

The Songs:

1. Jungleland
2. Lost in the Flood
3. Downbound Train
4. Drive All Night
5. Adam Raised a Cain
6. Factory
7. Open All Night
8. Crush on You
9. My Father's House
10. The Angel
11. Kitty's Back
12. Streets of Fire
13. She's the One
14. New York City Serenade
15. Seeds

The Albums:

A. Greetings from Asbury Park, N.J.

B. The Wild, the Innocent and the E Street Shuffle

C. Born to Run

D. Darkness on the Edge of Town

E. The River

F. Nebraska

G. Born in the U.S.A.

H. Bruce Springsteen & the E Street Band Live / 1975 - 85

(Answers on page 68.)

(photo: Debra Rothenberg)

Fill in the Blanks #1

— Released Songs —

Fill in the blanks to complete the titles of these officially released Springsteen songs:

1. My _____ House

2. Candy's _____

3. Because the _____

4. _____ by the Light

5. Fourth of July, _____ Park (Sandy)

6. _____ Day

7. The _____ Land

8. Mary Queen of _____

9. _____ It All Night

10. The _____ That _____

11. Streets of _____

12. _____ to Run

13. Two _____

14. Wild _____ Circus Story

15. Spirit in the _____

16. _____ on It

17. Out in the _____

18. Shut Out the _____

19. Meeting _____ the River

20. _____ Don't You Lose Heart

(Answers on page 69.)

(photo: John Corio)

Song Search #1

She's the One

In the following groups, three of the songs are from the same album, and one is not. Pick the song that doesn't belong.

1. Born to Run
   Thunder Road
   Kitty's Back
   Jungleland

2. Sherry Darling
   My Hometown
   Out in the Street
   Drive All Night

3. Wild Billy's Circus
      Story
   Spirit in the Night
   The Angel
   Mary Queen of
      Arkansas

4. War
   Prove It All Night
   Fire
   Raise Your Hand

5. No Surrender
   Cover Me
   I'm on Fire
   Badlands

6. Incident on 57th Street
   Rosalita (Come Out
      Tonight)
   For You
   Fourth of July, Asbury
      Park (Sandy)

7. The Promised Land
   Prove It All Night
   Factory
   She's the One

8. Atlantic City
   Reason to Believe
   Drive All Night
   Mansion on the Hill

(Answers on page 70.)

Glory Dates #1

— Guest Appearances —

Bruce often makes guest appearances with other bands, ranging from unknown groups at small clubs to headline acts at arenas. In the quiz below, match Bruce's guest appearance with the song(s) he sang:

The Appearances:

1. April 17, 1977 at the Stone Pony in Asbury Park, New Jersey, with Southside Johnny

2. December 2, 1977 at the NYU Student Center in New York City, with Robert Gordon and Link Wray

3. December 30, 1977 at CBGB's in New York City, with Patti Smith

4. August 25, 1978 at Toad's Place in New Haven, Conn., with Beaver Brown

5. May 1, 1981 at the Forum in Copenhagen, with Malurt

6. June 15, 1981 at the Old Waldorf in San Francisco, with Gary U.S. Bonds

7. September 5, 1981 at Perkin's Cow Palace in Pasadena, Calif., with the Pretenders

8.   September 21, 1982 at the Peppermint Lounge in New York City, with Dave Edmunds

9.   August 2, 1983 at Madison Square Garden in New York City, with Jackson Browne

10.   January 14, 1984 at Patrix in New Brunswick, New Jersey, with John Eddie and the Front Street Runners

11.   April 22, 1984 at the Stone Pony in Asbury Park, New Jersey, with Cats on a Smooth Surface

12.   August 22, 1984 at the Stone Pony in Asbury Park, New Jersey, with La Bamba and the Hubcaps

13.   January 17, 1985 at the Rhinoceros Club in Greensboro, North Carolina, with the Del Fuegos

14.   March 22, 1985 at the Entertainment Center in Sydney, Australia, with Neil Young

John Eddie and Max Weinberg at the Stone Pony
(photo: Debra Rothenberg)

The Songs:

A. Heartbreak Hotel

B. Higher and Higher

C. Route 66, In the Midnight Hour

D. Hungry Heart

E. Jole Blon, This Little Girl, Quarter to Three

F. Rosalita, Double Shot of My Baby's Love, You Can't Sit Down

G. Because the Night

H. From Small Things, Big Things One Day Come

I. Hang on Sloopy, Stand By Me

J. The Fever, I Don't Want to Go Home, You Mean So Much to Me

K. Stay, Sweet Little Sixteen, Running on Empty

L. Rockin' All Over the World, Ain't Too Proud to Beg, Boom Boom, Proud Mary, Twist and Shout, Hang on Sloopy

M. I'm Bad, I'm Nationwide, Little Latin Lupe Lu, Jersey Girl

N. Down by the River

O. Travelin' Band, I'm Bad, I'm Nationwide

(Answers on page 71.)

Cover Me Quiz #1

— *I'm a Rocker, Too* —

Many singers and bands have recorded Bruce Springsteen songs. Bruce himself has released some of these songs, while some of them remain unreleased. In some cases, Bruce wrote the song especially for the artist. In the quiz below, match the Springsteen song to the artist who covered it. (Some of the artists are very obscure!)

The Songs:

1. *Because the Night*
2. *Born to Run*
3. *Factory*
4. *The Fever*
5. *For You*
6. *From Small Things, Big Things One Day Come*
7. *Fire*
8. *Growin' Up*
9. *Hearts of Stone*

The Artists:

A. The Flying Pickets

B. Alvin Stardust

C. Dave Edmunds

D. Clarence Clemons and the Red Bank Rockers

E. ½ Japanese

F. Donna Summer

G. Dick Tool Company

H. Roger Taylor

I. Greg Kihn

10.	*Hungry Heart*	J.	Little Bob Story
11.	*If I Was the Priest*	K.	Andy Hamilton
12.	*Johnny 99*	L.	Emmylou Harris
13.	*The Price You Pay*	M.	Alan Rich
14.	*Protection*	N.	Johnny Cash
15.	*Racing in the Street*	O.	Southside Johnny and the Asbury Jukes
16.	*Savin' Up*		
17.	*Seaside Bar Song*	P.	Allan Clarke
18.	*Streets of Fire*	Q.	Frankie Goes to Hollywood
19.	*Tenth Avenue Freeze-out*	R.	Robert Gordon
		S.	Patti Smith

(Answers on page 71.)

Bonus Question #2

Name the three songs where Bruce mentions beer.

Answer: "Blinded by the Light," "Jungleland," and "Sherry Darling."

Bruce and Steven   (photo: Debra Rothenberg)

Q and A #2

— The Songs —

1. Bruce wrote the song "Fire" for another singer. Whom was it written for?

2. Name four New York City streets that are mentioned in Bruce's songs.

3. What song did Bruce co-write with Warren Zevon?

4. What Bruce song was released in Europe as a B-side, but was never released in the U.S.?

5. What song on Bruce's first album, *Greetings from Asbury Park, N.J.*, was a #1 hit?

6. Name four Bruce songs that have been released as music videos.

7. Name two songs which Bruce did not write that have been officially released by Bruce.

8. What was the B-side of Bruce's first single?

9. Name three of the twelve songs that Bruce made for the CBS demos in 1972.

10. How high on the charts did "Born to Run" get?

11. What live instrumental was issued on tape on a limited basis to radio stations in 1978?

12. Name four of the eight singles that Bruce released before *Born in the U.S.A.*

13. Name four Bruce songs that appear on albums by Gary U.S. Bonds.

14. What songs constitute the "Detroit Medley"?

15. What Springsteen-sung song was Bruce's first Top Ten hit?

16. What movie inspired the song "Nebraska"?

17. Who sings background vocals on "Thunder Road"?

18. Who plays the coronet on "The E Street Shuffle"?

19. What guest back-up singers are on the songs "No Surrender" and "My Hometown"?

(Answers on page 72.)

What happened " 'neath that giant Exxon sign"?
(photo: John Corio)

Match-Up Quiz #2

—— Drive All Night ——

Cars figure prominently in Bruce's lyrics. In the quiz below, match the car to the Springsteen song in which it appears:

The Cars:

1. Dodge
2. Buick
3. Camero
4. Batmobile
5. '32 Ford
6. Trans-Am
7. Volkswagen
8. Chevrolet

The Songs:

A. Cadillac Ranch
B. The Angel
C. Jungleland
D. I'm a Rocker
E. My Hometown
F. Thunder Road
G. Racing in the Street
H. Ramrod

(Answers on page 74.)

Bonus Question #3

What is the only foreign phrase in Bruce's lyrics?

Answer: "c'est magnifique" from "Crush on You"

Q and A #3

The Albums

1. What is the first line of the first song on Bruce's first album?

2. Who produced the first album?

3. Where was the album *Nebraska* recorded?

4. Which album does not include a lyric sheet?

5. Who took the photograph of Bruce for the cover of *Darkness on the Edge of Town*?

6. What singles were released in the U.S. from *The Wild, the Innocent and the E Street Shuffle*?

7. Name five songs that appear on the B-sides of singles but not on any album.

8. What Italian words appear on the album sleeve of *Born in the U.S.A.*?

9. Name the release date of each album.

10. Who has barefeet in the picture on the back cover of *The Wild, the Innocent and the E Street Shuffle*?

11. Which album has the fewest number of songs?

12. Which album has spawned the most singles?

(photo: Debra Rothenberg)

13. What album does not carry a producer credit?

14. What guest musicians appear on *Born to Run*?

15. What album cover, when first printed, misspelled Jon Landau's name?

(*Answers on page 75.*)

Match-Up Quiz #3

— Where the Bands Are —

Match these roads, places, and stores to the Springsteen songs in which they appear:

The Places:

1. Abram's Bridge
2. Khe Sahn
3. Wyoming
4. Sacred Heart
5. St. Mary's Gate
6. Baltimore
7. Seven-Eleven
8. Eldridge Avenue
9. Kingsley
10. Bluebird Street
11. Mahwah
12. Highway 95
13. Chelsea

The Songs:

A. Independence Day
B. Cadillac Ranch
C. Lost in the Flood
D. Stolen Car
E. Used Cars
F. Ramrod
G. Nebraska
H. Blinded By the Light
I. Johnny 99
J. Mansion on the Hill
K. Backstreets
L. Hungry Heart
M. Darkness on the Edge of Town

14.	Bob's Big Boy	N.	*Sherry Darling*
15.	Scotland Yard	O.	*For You*
16.	Linden Town	P.	*Rosalita*
17.	Michigan Avenue	Q.	*Racing in the Street*
18.	Woolworth's	R.	*Working on the Highway*
19.	Route 9	S.	*Something in the Night*
20.	Stockton's Wing	T.	*Born in the U.S.A.*
21.	The Vatican	U.	*Open All Night*
22.	Wisconsin	V.	*Born to Run*

(Answers on page 77.)

Bonus Question #4

What is the only newspaper mentioned in Bruce's lyrics?

Answer: The Daily News

During "Santa Claus Is Coming to Town"
(photo: Nancy Barr)

Glory Dates #2

Surprise Guests

Many singers have shown up at Springsteen concerts and performed a song or two with Bruce. In the quiz below, match the guest to the date and place that he or she appeared:

The Guests:

1. Bob Seger
2. Gary U. S. Bonds
3. John Entwhistle
4. J. T. Bowen
5. Eddie Floyd
6. Boz Scaggs
7. Patti Smith
8. Gary Busey
9. Jackson Browne
10. Link Wray
11. Pete Townshend
12. Tom Waits

The Appearances:

A. E. Rutherford—8/11/84
B. London—6/7/81
C. Philadelphia—8/18-19/78
D. Los Angeles—8/24/81
E. New Orleans—10/6/75
F. E. Rutherford—7/3/81
G. New York—10/30/76
H. Ann Arbor—10/3/80
I. Los Angeles—11/1/80
J. E. Rutherford—8/9/84
K. Memphis—4/28/76
L. London—6/2/81

(Answers on page 76.)

Song Search #2

Lost in the Flood

Can you find these Bruce songs in the puzzle below? (Note: Titles that are more than one word run together, so, for example, The Angel appears in the puzzle as THEANGEL.)

THE ANGEL
FOR YOU
KITTY'S BACK
ROSALITA
THUNDER ROAD
BACKSTREETS
BADLANDS
FACTORY

FIRE
BE TRUE
THE RIVER
RAMROD
NEBRASKA
USED CARS
COVER ME
GLORY DAYS

```
A  C  K  C  A  B  S  Y  T  T  I  K  L
T  D  R  I  E  H  T  R  E  A  R  S  E
H  H  O  M  T  S  A  R  B  E  H  T  G
E  T  U  R  B  A  K  S  A  R  B  E  N
R  A  M  N  M  R  T  Y  T  S  E  E  A
I  L  P  Y  D  A  Y  A  I  D  T  R  E
V  B  O  S  K  E  R  D  L  N  R  T  H
E  F  A  C  T  O  R  Y  A  A  U  S  T
R  O  I  J  G  I  L  R  S  L  E  K  L
O  R  N  R  R  T  H  O  O  D  R  C  O
T  Y  T  E  E  R  I  L  R  A  V  A  J
C  O  V  E  R  M  E  G  O  B  D  B  A
F  U  S  E  D  C  A  R  S  E  V  O  C
```

(Answers on page 77.)

Match-Up Quiz #4

— The Working Life —

In the following Bruce songs, the characters have specific jobs. Match the song with its character's job or place of work.

The Songs:

1. The Promised Land
2. Open All Night
3. Downbound Train
4. Out in the Street
5. Working on the Highway
6. The River
7. Highway Patrolman

Where They Work:

A. on Highway 95

B. construction for the Johnstown Company

C. loading crates on the dock

D. in daddy's garage

E. police sargent

F. counter girl at Bob's Big Boy

G. at the car wash

(Answers on page 78.)

Cover Me Quiz #2

-This Song Is Your Song-

As far as we know, Bruce has performed a "cover" of each
of these songs only once. Match the song with the date
and place of that rare performance:

The Songs:

1. Chimes of Freedom
2. Deportee
3. Haunted House
4. He's Sure the Boy I Love
5. I Sold My Heart to the Junkman
6. Knock on Wood
7. Memphis
8. Mystery Train
9. Night Train
10. Nothing's Too Good for My Baby
11. Oh Boy
12. On Top of Old Smokey
13. Outer Limits
14. Sea Cruise
15. 634-5789
16. Take Me Out to the Ballgame
17. Tutti Frutti
18. Uptight (Everything's Alright)
19. Waltz Across Texas
20. Wabash Cannonball
21. Woman's Got the Power
22. Yum Yum, I Want Some

Where and When Played:

A. Atlanta, GA—September 30, 1978

B. Memphis, TN—April 28, 1976

C. New York, NY—November 28, 1980

D. St. Petersburg, FL—July 29, 1978

E. Los Angeles, CA—October 31, 1980

F. Cambridge, MA—May 9, 1974

G. Memphis, TN—December 13, 1984

H. Portland, OR—October 25, 1980

I. Houston, TX—September 13, 1975

J. Detroit, MI—September 1, 1978

K. Binghamton, NY—June 12, 1973

L. Los Angeles, CA—August 28, 1981

M. Parsippany, NJ—January 12, 1974

N. Los Angeles, CA—October 31, 1980

O. Denver, CO—August 16, 1981

P. East Rutherford, NJ—August 9, 1984

Q. Los Angeles, CA—November 1, 1980

R. Neptune, NJ—July 16, 1983

S. Philadelphia, PA—December 6, 1980

T. Austin, TX—November 9, 1980

U. Red Bank, NJ—August 1, 1976

V. Memphis, TN—April 29, 1976

(Answers on page 78.)

(photo: Nancy Barr)

Q and A #4

The Characters

1. Who said "You've got a lot to learn . . ."?

2. Who is the hero of "Incident on 57th Street"?

3. Name ten women in Bruce's songs (first names only).

4. Who "rides to heaven on a gyroscope"?

5. Who is Joe Roberts' brother?

6. Who went to Greasy Lake?

7. Where did Magic Rat drive his sleek machine?

8. Where did "me and Terry" sleep?

9. Where did they blow up the Chicken Man?

10. Where is the '69 Chevy with a 396 waiting?

11. Where did they slap the cuffs on Johnny 99?

12. In "Thunder Road," who sings for the lonely?

13. What do the poets in Jungleland do?

14. Where did Spanish Johnny drive in from?

15. Where did he try to sell his heart?

16. What did Rosalita's boyfriend get from the record company?

17. What is the price you've gotta pay in "Badlands"?

18. How many innocent people died in "Nebraska"?

19. Where was the auto plant that closed, leaving Johnny 99 unemployed?

20. What are on the walls in Candy's room?

21. How far did Wayne and his friend drive to get to Darlington County?

22. What is Johnny 99's real name?

23. In "The River," where did the boy and girl meet?

24. What was knocked over in "You Can Look (But You Better Not Touch)"?

25. What did Johnny 99 get drunk on?

26. Where are the characters going to drive in "Prove It All Night"?

27. Where did Wayne and his buddy come from in "Darlington County"?

28. How much money do they have?

29. Where does Wayne's buddy leave him?

30. Who was the judge at Johnny 99's trial?

31. When did the characters in "Bobby Jean" become friends?

32. When did Joe Roberts' brother go into the army?

33. What is closing down in "My Hometown"?

34. Where does Sherry's mother have to be driven?

35. What was the little sister eating in "Used Cars"?

36. What can't you start a fire without?

37. What was the name of the baby baptized in "Reason to Believe"?

38. Where is the party "Out in the Street"?

39. What did the man in "The River" get for his 19th birthday?

40. Who is going to go along to the Cadillac Ranch?

41. What did Queen Isabella tell Columbus?

42. In "Be True," what is the girl's scrapbook filled with?

(Answers on page 79.)

Bonus Question #5

How many Springsteen compact discs exist?

Answer: 11

Joe Piscopo imitates The Boss.

(photo: Debra Rothenberg)

Glory Dates #3

The Concerts

1. In what midwestern town was a Springsteen concert delayed in 1975 because of a bomb scare?

2. When the show resumed, with what song did Bruce open?

3. Where did Bruce perform the night that Jon Landau was inspired to write, "I saw rock 'n roll future and its name is Bruce Springsteen."

4. For whom did Bruce open at the Schaefer Music Festival in August, 1974?

5. When did Bruce first perform in an arena?

6. What is the only released Springsteen song that he has never performed in a concert?

7. Where and when did Bruce perform the only live version of "Be True"?

8. What New York club did Bruce play frequently with The Castiles in January and February of 1966?

9. What song did Bruce open with on the first night of his famous shows at the Bottom Line in August, 1975?

10. What appropriate song did Bruce close with on January 27, 1985, his last show in the U.S. before the European leg of the "Born in the U.S.A." tour?

11. The day Bruce auditioned for John Hammond, Hammond arranged for him to perform that night at a Greenwich Village nightclub. What club was that?

12. Bruce played a benefit at Charley's in Boston in April, 1974. Whom was the benefit for?

13. When Bruce first played London in 1975, he ran around ripping down posters with a slogan printed on them. What did the posters say?

14. What Bob Dylan song did Bruce cover in Philadelphia and elsewhere, featuring a violin?

15. When and where was the live premiere of "Stand on It"?

16. What original, unrecorded songs did Bruce premiere during the "Born in the U.S.A." tour?

17. When and where did the "Born in the U.S.A." tour begin?

18. When was Bruce's first ballpark concert?

19. When Bruce opened the Byrne Arena in East Rutherford, New Jersey in 1981, how many shows did he play?

20. What were the dates of those shows?

21. When was Bruce's first concert in Japan?

22. What countries did the "Born in the U.S.A." tour cover?

Bruce and his sister Ginny, "Dancing in the Dark"
(photo: Debra Rothenberg)

23. During which songs has Bruce pulled girls from the audience to dance with him?

24. Where was the live premiere of "Dancing in the Dark"?

25. When was the first show in over ten years that did not include "Rosalita"?

(Answers on page 81.)

Fill in the Blanks #2

— *Unreleased Songs* —

Fill in the blanks to complete the titles of these unreleased
Springsteen songs:

1. Zero and _____ Terry

2. _____ of the Sea

3. That's _____ You Get

4. Down by the _____

5. A _____ So Fine

6. Hey Santa _____

7. _____ Let Me Be the One

8. Action in the _____

9. _____ Look Back

10. City at _____

11. _____ at Fort Horne

12. Where the _____ Are

13. Two _____ in True Waltz Time

14. _____ Ends

15. Murder, _____

16. My _____ Won't Let _____ Down

17. The _____ Daughter

18. _____ Bar Song

19. _____ Them As They _____

20. This _____ Land

(Answers on page 84.)

(photo: Steve Zuckerman)

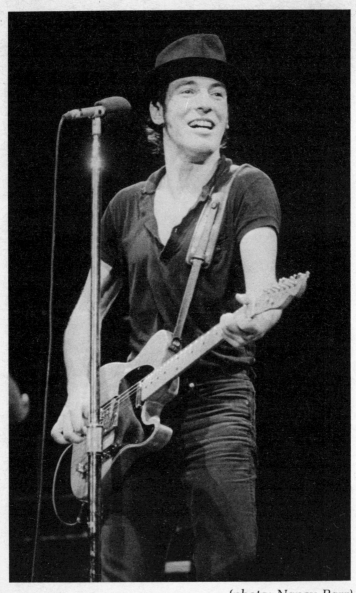

(photo: Nancy Barr)

Q and A #5

— Unreleased Songs —

1. What incident inspired "Roulette"?

2. What song was removed from *Darkness on the Edge of Town* at the last minute?

3. What song was originally recorded for *Darkness on the Edge of Town* but not released, and then re-recorded for *Born in the U.S.A.* and again not released?

4. What song features the line, "Are you alive"?

5. Why was the song "The Promise" left off *Darkness on the Edge of Town* ?

6. When "Cindy" is picked up at work, what is she brought?

7. Who wants a man of her own?

8. Who has the heart of a ballerina?

9. In what song do Frank and his brother look for lost cattle?

10. From what song does the tune at the end of "Thunder Road" come from?

11. What car was sold in "The Promise"?

12. What was left in the yard in "Roulette"?

13. In what song is the listener told to get in his wheels and roll?

14. What unreleased song is also known as "Contessa" or "Guns of Kid Cole"?

15. Where are the bands ringing in "Where the Bands Are"?

16. What color are the eyes of the girl in "My Love Won't Let You Down"?

17. What song, performed only once, was the predecessor to "Zero and Blind Terry"?

18. In "The Promise," what do the characters Johnny, Billy, and Terry do?

19. What does the Virgin Mary run in "If I Was the Priest"?

20. What does the little boy watch in "Hey Santa Ana"?

(Answers on page 85.)

Bonus Question #6

What three songs contain the word "backstreets"?

Answer: "It's Hard to Be a Saint in the City," "Jungleland," and "Backstreets."

Match-Up Quiz #5

——— Saints in the City ———

Match these famous people to the songs in which they appear:

The People:

1. Joan Fontaine
2. Roy Orbison
3. Mozart
4. Burt Reynolds
5. James Bond
6. Brando
7. Columbus
8. Adam and Eve

(Answers on page 86.)

The Songs:

A. Thunder Road

B. It's Hard to Be a Saint in the City

C. Does This Bus Stop at 82nd Street?

D. Cadillac Ranch

E. I'm a Rocker

F. Blinded by the Light

G. Pink Cadillac

H. Stand on It

Bonus Question #7

Where can you find "the key to the universe"?

Answer: "in the engine of an old parked car."

Q and A #6

The Band

1. Four women have shared the stage with Bruce as members of his band. Name two of them.

2. What is the only song that Ernest "Boom" Carter played on?

3. Name three members of the band Steel Mill.

4. What Bruce band featured a Monopoly board?

5. At the CBS Records convention in July 1973, what act did Bruce follow?

6. When did Ernest "Boom" Carter make his first appearance with the band?

7. Where did Bruce and Roy Bittan first meet?

8. In what Broadway show's road tour did Roy play?

9. At what sports event did Clarence Clemons perform the National Anthem?

10. When Clarence's band played at the Stone Pony in Asbury Park on May 19, 1984, Bruce joined them for the last four songs. Name two of them.

11. Where were Clarence and Bruce playing the night they met?

Clarence, Bruce, Garry, Steven and Max on drums.
(photo: David Denenberg)

12. How old was Clarence when he got his first saxophone?

13. What was the name of Danny Federici's first band?

14. What did Bruce give Danny onstage at the Los Angeles concert on October 31, 1984?

15. Who was the manager of Danny's high school band, The Legends?

16. What acrobatic act did Nils Lofgren perform during part of the "Born in the U.S.A." tour?

17. Where did both Bruce and Nils audition on the same night in 1969?

18. What was Nils' vinyl debut with the E Street Band?

19. Where did Bruce find Patti Scialfa?

20. What former member of the E Street Band did Patti record with?

21. What day did Patti officially join the band?

22. What kind of jukebox does Garry Tallent own?

23. What credit does Garry receive on Clarence Clemon's album, *Rescue* ?

24. What contribution did Steve Van Zandt make to Bruce's first album?

25. What are the titles of Steve's solo albums?

26. Name three nicknames Steve has used.

27. Which of Bruce's albums did Steve co-produce?

28. With whom did Max Weinberg study the drums?

29. What book did Max write?

30. In what orchestras of Broadway shows did Max play?

(Answers on page 87.)

Bonus Question #8

What three songs have parentheses in their title?

Answer: "4th of July, Asbury Park (Sandy)," "Rosalita (Come Out Tonight)," and "You Can Look (But You Better Not Touch)."

Garry Tallent
(photos: Debra
Rothenberg)

Nils Lofgren

Match-Up Quiz #6

The E Streeters

Match the band member with his or her nickname:

The Band:

1. Roy Bittan
2. Ernest Carter
3. Clarence Clemons
4. Danny Federici
5. Nils Lofgren
6. Vini Lopez
7. Patti Scialfa
8. Bruce Springsteen
9. Garry Tallent
10. Steve Van Zandt
11. Max Weinberg

The Nicknames:

A. Mad Dog
B. Boom
C. The Professor
D. Funky
E. Phantom
F. Miami
G. Lefty
H. Big Man
I. The Boss
J. Red
K. Mighty

(Answers on page 89.)

(photo: Nancy Barr)

Match-Up Quiz #7

My Hometown

Match the member of Bruce's band to his or her hometown:

Band Members:

1. Roy Bittan
2. Clarence Clemons
3. Danny Federici
4. Nils Lofgren
5. Vini Lopez
6. David Sancious
7. Patti Scialfa
8. Bruce Springsteen
9. Garry Tallent
10. Steve Van Zandt
11. Max Weinberg

Hometowns:

A. Belmar, NJ
B. Deal, NJ
C. South Orange, NJ
D. Freehold, NJ
E. Rockaway Beach, NY
F. Flemington, NJ
G. Detroit, Michigan
H. Chicago, Illinois
I. Norfolk, Virginia
J. Winthrop, Mass
K. Neptune, NJ

(Answers on page 90.)

Bonus Question #9

What is the only official Springsteen release containing nothing written by Bruce?

Answer: The single with "War" on Side A and "Merry Christmas Baby" on Side B.

Bonus Question #10

What is the only song title with a hyphen?

Answer: "Tenth Avenue Freeze-Out"

Match-Up Quiz #8

—*The Songs That Bind*—

Match the opening song of each album to the song that closes the album:

Opening Songs:

1. Badlands

2. Blinded by the Light

3. Born in the U.S.A.

4. The Ties That Bind

5. Thunder Road

6. Nebraska

7. The E Street Shuffle

Closing Songs:

A. Reason to Believe

B. New York City Serenade

C. Darkness on the Edge of Town

D. Wreck on the Highway

E. My Hometown

F. It's Hard to Be a Saint in the City

G. Jungleland

H. Jersey Girl

(Answers on page 90.)

Q and A #7

Miscellaneous

1. What California DJ did Bruce ask for a date while on the air in July, 1978?

2. Who were the managers of each of Bruce's bands?

3. Prior to Bruce, what was Mike Appel's musical affiliation?

4. What song did Bruce tell John Hammond he would never perform live?

5. What Boston paper did Jon Landau write for prior to his managing Bruce?

6. On what day did Bruce audition for CBS talent scout John Hammond?

7. When did Bruce sign a recording contract with CBS Records?

8. How did Bruce know who John Hammond was?

9. What did Mike Appel want Bruce to sing at the Super Bowl in 1972?

10. What reviewer said, "I have never been so overwhelmed by an unknown band."?

11. To what band was he referring?

12. What day was the legendary quote "I saw rock and roll future and its name is Bruce Springsteen" published?

13. Where and when did Bruce first meet Jon Landau?

14. When was the "Rosalita" video filmed?

15. When did Bruce climb over the gate at Graceland in an attempt to meet Elvis Presley?

16. What was the date of the issues of *Time* and *Newsweek* that both featured Bruce on the cover in the same week?

17. What did *Newsweek* title its cover story on Bruce?

18. What song did DJ Kid Leo of WMMS-FM in Cleveland play during part of 1975 every Friday at 5:55 to launch the weekend?

19. What videos, other than his own, does Bruce appear in?

20. What American movies feature Springsteen songs?

21. Which songs were used in these movies?

22. Where is the real Cadillac Ranch located?

23. Where did Bruce celebrate his 35th birthday?

24. Who is the actress Bruce pulls up on stage during the "Dancing in the Dark" video?

25. In what category did Bruce win a Grammy Award?

26. Who directed the *first* "Dancing in the Dark" video?

27. What songs does Bruce perform in the film, *No Nukes?*

28. When the B-side song "Be True" was first issued, there was a misprint on the record. What was the misprint?

29. What does Bruce do in Clarence Clemons' video, "Woman's Got the Power"?

30. Who is the luthier who repairs Bruce's guitar?
(Answers on page 91.)

Clarence and Bruce taking a break onstage.

(photo: Nancy Barr)

Match-Up Quiz #9

B True

Match the A-side of each single to its B-side:

A-Sides:

1. Blinded by the Light
2. Spirit in the Night
3. Born to Run
4. Tenth Avenue Freeze-Out
5. Prove It All Night
6. Badlands
7. Hungry Heart
8. Fade Away
9. Dancing in the Dark
10. Cover Me
11. I'm on Fire
12. Glory Days
13. I'm Going Down
14. My Hometown

B-Sides:

A. Johnny Bye Bye
B. Meeting Across the River
C. Janey Don't You Lose Heart
D. Factory
E. The Angel
F. Pink Cadillac
G. Held Up Without a Gun
H. Jersey Girl
I. For You
J. She's the One
K. Stand on It
L. Streets of Fire
M. Be True
N. Santa Claus Is Coming to Town

(Answers on page 94.)

Bruce and Robert Gordon singing "Fire"
(photo courtesy RCA Records)

Bonus Question #11

Approximately how many times does Bruce sing the words "little girl" in his first seven albums?

Answer: According to our unscientific count, 29.

Bonus Question #12: Who's the woman with Bruce, and why is she in this book?

(photo: Barb Kinney/USA Today)

Answer: That's actress Julianne Phillips, who married Bruce on May 13, 1985 in Lake Oswego, OR.

The Answers

Q and A #1
Growin' Up

1. Bruce attended Saint Rose of Lima.

2. Bruce's first band was The Castiles, named after the soap the lead singer used on his hair. The band was popular in New Jersey and played mostly covers and some original material.

3. George Theiss, the band's lead singer. Theiss was dating Bruce's younger sister, Ginny, and when The Castiles had an opening for a guitarist, Bruce was invited to audition for the spot.

4. A recording booth in the Brick Mall Shopping Center in Bricktown, New Jersey.

5. "That's What You Get" and "Baby I," which were co-written by Springsteen and Theiss.

6. The time cost $50 per hour.

7. While recording, Bruce's E-string broke. Since they only had an hour, he finished recording without it.

8. Bruce Springsteen, George Theiss (lead vocals and rhythm guitar), Curt Fluhr (bass), Paul Popkin (tambourine and vocals), Bob Alfano (organ), and Bart Haynes (drums), who was replaced by Vince Manniello.

9. Ducky Slattery. He got his nickname from the Marx Brothers' joke he often repeated: "Wanna buy a duck?"

10. Bruce spent one very unhappy semester studying at Ocean County Community College.

11. Bruce had poetry published in the school's literary magazine.

12. Bruce's sisters are Virginia ("Ginny") and Pamela.

13. Adele Zirilli

14. Adele was a secretary.

15. When Bruce was eight, he saw Elvis Presley on *The Ed Sullivan Show* and decided he wanted to be Elvis.

16. E Street and Tenth Avenue are located in the shore town of Belmar, New Jersey.

17. David Sancious, the former E Street Band pianist. Sancious lived with his parents on the corner of E Street and Tenth Avenue in Belmar. The band in its early days used to rehearse in the basement of the Sancious' house, thus the name "The E Street Band."

18. Immortalized in the song "Fourth of July, Asbury Park (Sandy)," Madame Marie still tells fortunes on the boardwalk in Asbury Park.

19. Tom and Margaret Potter ran the Upstage in Asbury Park, a popular hangout for musicians. It's where Bruce first met and played with Steve Van Zandt, Southside Johnny, Garry Tallent, and many other local musicians.

20. The manager of Steel Mill, Tinker West, taught Bruce to drive during a trip the band made to California.

21. His guitar came from a pawnshop.

22. It cost $18.

23. His cousin Frankie taught him his first chords.

24. Because Tex Vinyard, the manager of The Castiles, was on strike from his factory job.

25. He got $21 a week in union benefits.

26. The Castiles' first gig was at the West Haven (New Jersey) Swim Club.

27. They were paid $35.

28. They closed with a favorite number of Tex's, "In the Mood" by Glenn Miller, arranged by Bruce.

29. George Theiss, leader of The Castiles, had a crush on Bruce's younger sister, Ginny, and would go over to the Springsteen's house to see her.

30. Tex told Bruce to come back after he learned four or five songs.

Match-Up Quiz #1
On the Backstreets

1. C	6. D	11. B
2. A	7. F	12. D
3. G	8. E	13. C
4. E	9. F	14. B
5. D and H	10. A	15. H

Fill in the Blanks #1
Released Songs

1. My **Father's** House

2. Candy's **Room**

3. Because the **Night**

4. **Blinded** by the Light

5. Fourth of July, **Asbury** Park (Sandy)

6. **Independence** Day

7. The **Promised** Land

8. Mary Queen of **Arkansas**

9. **Prove** It All Night

10. The **Ties** That **Bind**

11. Streets of **Fire**

12. **Born** to Run

13. Two **Hearts**

14. Wild **Billy's** Circus Story

15. Spirit in the **Night**

16. **Stand** on It

17. Out in the **Street**

18. Shut Out the **Light**

19. Meeting **Across** the River

20. **Janey** Don't You Lose Heart

Song Search #1
She's the One

1. "Kitty's Back." The other songs are from *Born to Run.*

2. "My Hometown." The other songs are from *The River.*

3. "Wild Billy's Circus Story." The other songs are from *Greetings from Asbury Park, N.J.*

4. "Prove It All Night." The other songs are from *Bruce Springsteen & the E Street Band Live / 1975 - 85.*

5. "Badlands." The other songs are from *Born in the U.S.A.*

6. "For You." The other songs are from *The Wild, the Innocent and the E Street Shuffle.*

7. "She's the One." The other songs are from *Darkness on the Edge of Town.*

8. "Drive All Night." The other songs are from *Nebraska.*

Glory Dates #1
Guest Appearances

1. J
2. A
3. G
4. H
5. D
6. E
7. F
8. B
9. K
10. L
11. M
12. O
13. I
14. N

Cover Me Quiz #1
I'm a Rocker, Too

1. S
2. Q
3. A
4. M or O
5. I
6. C
7. R
8. B
9. O
10. K
11. P
12. N
13. L
14. F
15. H
16. D
17. J
18. G
19. E

Q and A #2
The Songs

1. Bruce wrote "Fire" for his idol, Elvis Presley. A few weeks before Elvis died in August, 1977, Bruce sent him a demo of the song, but Elvis never heard it.

2. Bleeker Street, 57th Street, 53rd Street, 82nd Street, Broadway, Madison Avenue, and 8th Avenue are mentioned in various songs. Tenth Avenue is also mentioned, but it refers to a street in Belmar, New Jersey.

3. Originally titled "Janey Needs a Shooter," the Zevon / Springsteen collaboration was almost entirely rewritten and called "Jeannie Needs a Shooter."

4. "The Big Payback," the B-side of the European single "Open All Night."

5. "Blinded by the Light" made #1 in 1976, but it was the version by Manfred Mann's Earth Band, not Bruce Springsteen, that topped the charts.

6. "Atlantic City," "Rosalita," "Dancing in the Dark," "Born in the U.S.A.," "I'm on Fire," "Glory Days," "My Hometown," and "War" have been produced as music videos as of this writing.

7. "Detroit Medley," "Jersey Girl," "Trapped," "Santa Claus Is Coming to Town," "War," "Merry Christmas Baby," "Raise Your Hand," and "This Land Is Your Land."

8. "The Angel."

9. "Mary Queen of Arkansas" (two takes), "It's Hard to Be a Saint in the City," "If I Was the Priest," "Southern Son," "Jazz Musician" (two takes), "Growin' Up," "Two Hearts in True Waltz Time," "Arabian Nights," "Street Queen," "The Angel," "Cowboys of the Sea," and "Does This Bus Stop at 82nd Street?"

10. "Born to Run" peaked at #18.

11. "Paradise by the 'C'," which often opened the second set of Bruce's concerts in 1978. The version issued was recorded at the Berkeley Community Theater.

12. "Blinded by the Light," "Spirit in the Night," "Born to Run," "Tenth Avenue Freeze-out," "Badlands," "Prove It All Night," "Hungry Heart," "Fade Away."

13. "This Little Girl," "Your Love," "Dedication," "Hold On (To What You Got)," "Out of Work," "Club Soul City," "Love's on the Line," "Rendezvous," "Angelyne," and "All I Need" are all Springsteen compositions that appear on Gary U.S. Bonds' albums, *Dedication* and *On the Line*.

14. Usually, the "Detroit Medley" consists of "Devil with the Blue Dress," "C. C. Rider," "Good Golly, Miss Molly," and "Jenny Take a Ride," with occasional additions of songs like "High School Confidential" and "Travelin' Band."

15. "Hungry Heart"

16. *Nebraska* was inspired by the film *Badlands*, about the Charles Starkweather/Caril Fugate murders.

17. Roy Bittan, Steve Van Zandt, and Mike Appel sing the background vocals.

18. Vini Lopez plays coronet.

19. The singers are La Bamba and Ruth Jackson.

Match-Up Quiz #2
Drive All Night

1. C
2. E
3. G
4. D
5. H
6. A
7. B
8. F

(photo: John Corio)

Q and A #3
The Albums

1. "Madman drummers bummers and Indians in the summer with a teenage diplomat..."

2. Mike Appel and Jim Cretecos

3. The album, originally planned as demos for the band, was recorded in Bruce's home in Holmdel, New Jersey.

4. *The Wild, the Innocent and the E Street Shuffle*. Springsteen has said that the biggest complaint he got about the album was that the lyrics were not included.

5. New Jersey photographer Frank Stefanko.

6. None, although "Rosalita (Come Out Tonight)" and "Fourth of July, Asbury Park (Sandy)" were later released in some European countries.

7. "Held Up Without a Gun," "Be True," "Pink Cadillac," "Jersey Girl," "Shut Out the Light," "Johnny Bye Bye," "Stand on It," "Janey Don't You Lose Heart," "Santa Claus Is Coming to Town," "Merry Christmas Baby," and, in Europe only, "The Big Payback." (Earlier B-sides were songs released on the albums, but it was with the singles from *The River* that Bruce began issuing B-sides that were otherwise unreleased.)

8. "*Buon viaggio, mio fratello*, Little Steven"

9. *Greetings from Asbury Park, N.J.*, January 5, 1973; *The Wild, the Innocent and the E Street Shuffle*, September 11, 1973; *Born to Run*, August 25, 1975; *Darkness on the Edge of Town*, June 2, 1978; *The River*, October 10, 1980; *Nebraska*, September 20, 1982; *Born in the U.S.A.*, June 4, 1984; *Bruce Springsteen & the E Street Band Live / 1975 - 85*, November 10, 1986.

10. Both Clarence Clemons and David Sancious have barefeet. Gary Tallent has one shoe on.

11. *The Wild, the Innocent and the E Street Shuffle* has only seven songs.

12. There were seven singles from *Born in the U.S.A.*

13. There is no producer credit listed on *Nebraska*.

14. Randy Brecker, Michael Brecker, Dave Sanborn, Wayne Andre, and Richard Davis.

15. Jon Landau's name was spelled "John" on the original printing of *Born to Run*.

Glory Dates #2
Surprise Guests

1. H		7. G	
2. F		8. C	
3. A		9. I	
4. J		10. L	
5. K		11. B	
6. E		12. D	

Match-Up Quiz #3
Where the Bands Are

1. M
2. T
3. G
4. N
5. A
6. L
7. Q

8. D
9. S
10. F
11. I
12. R
13. O
14. U
15. H

16. J
17. E
18. P
19. V
20. K
21. C
22. B

Song Search #2
Lost in the Flood

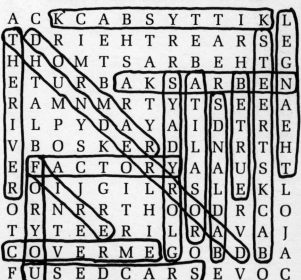

Match-Up Quiz #4
The Working Life

1. D
2. F
3. G
4. C
5. A
6. B
7. E

Cover Me Quiz #2
This Song Is Your Song

1. J
2. L
3. E
4. U
5. F
6. B
7. G
8. C
9. A
10. I
11. D

12. H
13. N
14. O
15. M
16. K
17. R
18. S
19. T
20. Q
21. P
22. V

Q and A #4
The Characters

1. Candy

2. Spanish Johnny

3. Annie, Candy, Cherry, Eve, Isabella, Jackie, Jane (Janey), Joan, Kate, Kitty, Margarita, Maria, Marie, Mary, Mary Beth, Mary Lou, Rosalita, Rose, Rosie, Sally, Sandy, Sheena, Sherry, Wanda, Wendy

4. Mary Lou

5. Franky

6. Crazy Janey, Wild Billy, Hazy Davey, and Killer Joe

7. over the Jersey state line

8. in that old abandoned beach house

9. Philly

10. outside the Seven-Eleven store

11. outside the Club Tip Top

12. Roy Orbison

13. They stand back and let it all be

14. from the underworld

15. on Easy Street

16. a big advance

17. the broken hearts

18. ten

19. Mahwah

20. pictures of her heroes

21. 800 miles

22. Ralph

23. high school

24. a lamp

25. Tanqueray and wine

26. from Monroe to Angeline

27. New York City

28. $200

29. handcuffed to a state trooper's Ford

30. Mean John Brown

31. when they were 16

32. 1965

33. the textile mill

34. to the unemployment agency

35. an ice cream cone

36. a spark

37. Kyle William

38. beneath the neon lights

39. a union card and a wedding coat

40. his pa and his aunt

41. "Stand on it!"

42. pictures of her leading men

Glory Dates #3
The Concerts

1. Milwaukee. He was playing at the Uptown Theater on October 2, 1975.

2. After spending the interim hours in a bar, a somewhat drunken Bruce re-opened the show with "Little Queenie," including a story about telling the bartender how "Somebody tried to blow us up tonight!"

3. Bruce was performing at the Harvard Square Theater in Cambridge on May 9, 1974. That night included the first live performance of the then-unreleased "Born to Run" and a cover version of "I Sold My Heart to the Junkman."

4. Anne Murray, who was greeted by fans screaming "We want Bruce!" She was not pleased.

5. Bruce first played an arena as the opening act for the band Chicago on May 31, 1973. The reception he received was so poor that he swore he would never again appear as an opening act, and he never has. As a headliner, his first arena show was at the Spectrum in Philadelphia on October 25, 1976.

6. "The Angel," released on Bruce's first album.

7. At the Capital Center in Largo, Maryland, on August 26, 1984. Before singing the song, Bruce dedicated it to Lisa Iannucci, "the girl who wrote the words down backstage."

8. The Castiles played 29 shows at the Cafe Wha in Greenwich Village.

9. He opened his first set at the Bottom Line with an acoustic version of the then-unreleased "Thunder Road."

10. Bruce ended the tour in Syracuse, New York, with the John Fogarty song, "Rockin' All Over the World."

11. Bruce performed at the Gaslight. Hammond arranged the performance with Sam Hood, the manager.

12. The benefit was for Joe Spadafora, who ran a club called Joe's Place in Boston. Bruce often played Joe's Place in his early days, and when Joe's burned down, the benefit was arranged.

13. "At Last London Is Ready for Bruce Springsteen!"

14. A slowed-down version of "I Want You."

15. "Stand on It" premiered at Giants Stadium, East Rutherford, New Jersey, on August 31, 1985. After all the encores were done, Bruce suddenly turned around and called out the song.

16. Bruce premiered the songs "Man at the Top," "Sugarland," and, during the latter part of the tour, "Seeds."

17. The "Born in the U.S.A." tour began in St. Paul, Minnesota on June 29, 1984.

18. Bruce's first ballpark show was at the CNE Grandstand in Toronto, Canada on July 23, 1984.

19. He played six shows.

20. July 2, 3, 5, 6, 8, and 9, 1981.

21. The band's first Japanese concert was April 8, 1985 at the Yoyogi Gym in Tokyo.

22. It covered Australia, Japan, Ireland, England, Sweden, The Netherlands, Germany, Italy, France, Canada, and, of course, the U.S.A.

23. During previous tours, Bruce would pull a girl up on stage to dance with him during the instrumental break in "Sherry Darling." However, he now brings up a dance partner at the end of "Dancing in the Dark."

24. "Dancing in the Dark" was first performed live by Bruce without the E Street Band. It was on May 26, 1984, during one of his surprise appearances, that he did the song with a band called Bystander at Club Xanadu in Asbury Park.

25. It was at the Tacoma Dome in Tacoma, Washington on October 19, 1984.

Fill in the Blanks #2
Unreleased Songs

1. Zero and **Blind** Terry

2. **Cowboys** of the Sea

3. That's **What** You Get

4. Down by the **River**

5. A **Love** So Fine

6. Hey Santa **Ana**

7. **Linda** Let Me Be the One

8. Action in the **Streets**

9. **Don't** Look Back

10. City at **Night**

11. **Visitation** at Fort Horne

12. Where the **Bands** Are

13. Two **Hearts** in True Waltz Time

14. **Loose** Ends

15. Murder, **Incorporated**

16. My **Love** Won't Let **You** Down

17. The **Preacher's** Daughter

18. **Seaside** Bar Song

19. **Take** Them as They **Come**

20. This **Hard** Land

Q and A #5
Unreleased Songs

1. The accident at the Three Mile Island nuclear power plant.

2. "Don't Look Back"

3. "Frankie"

4. "Action in the Streets"

5. Bruce felt that too many people thought it was about his lawsuit against Mike Appel. It wasn't.

6. Flowers

7. Rickie

8. The angel from the inner lake

9. "This Hard Land"

10. "Walking in the Street." Early versions of "Thunder Road" have either no sax at the end or a different tune.

11. A Challenger

12. Toys

13. "Seaside Bar Song"

14. "Hey Santa Ana"

15. They're ringing down Union Street

16. Blue

17. "Over the Hills of Saint Croix"

18. Johnny works in a factory, Billy works downtown, and Terry works in a rock and roll band.

19. The Holy Grail Saloon

20. The procession through town

Match-Up Quiz #5
Saints in the City

1. C   5. E

2. A   6. B

3. F   7. H

4. D   8. G

Bonus Question #13

The *Asbury Park Press* put the news of Bruce's marriage on page 1. What was the first line of that story?

Answer: "You could almost hear the sound of hearts breaking all along the Jersey Shore."

Q and A #6
The Band

1. Patti Scialfa, Suki Lahav, Francine Daniels, and Delores Holmes. Daniels and Holmes sang with two of Bruce's early bands, The Bruce Springsteen Band and Dr. Zoom and the Sonic Boom.

2. Carter played drums on "Born to Run."

3. At various times, Bruce, Steve Van Zandt, Danny Federici, Vini Roslyn, Robbin Thompson, and Vini Lopez comprised the band Steel Mill.

4. The short-lived Dr. Zoom and the Sonic Boom featured a Monopoly board. People who didn't know how to play an instrument would play the board so they could say they were in the band.

5. Bruce followed Edgar Winter.

6. Ernest "Boom" Carter first appeared with the band at the Satellite Lounge in Cookstown, New Jersey, on February 23, 1974.

7. Bruce and Roy met backstage at Max's Kansas City, a club in New York City.

8. He toured with "Jesus Christ Superstar."

9. The Knicks vs. Lakers at Madison Square Garden, January 3, 1984.

10. Bruce surprised the crowd at the Stone Pony by showing up to play "Fire," "In the Midnight Hour," "Lucille," and "Twist and Shout."

11. The night they met, both were playing in Asbury Park—Clarence at the Wonder Bar and Bruce at the Student Prince.

12. When Clarence was nine, his father bought him his first saxophone.

13. Danny's first band was called The Dan Federici Experience.

14. In honor of Danny's playing with the band for 15 years, Bruce presented him with a washing machine.

15. They were managed by Danny's mother.

16. During the early part of the tour, Nils did a back-flip.

17. Bruce and Nils were both auditioning at the Fillmore West in San Francisco.

18. "Trapped" was the first recorded release of the band that includes Nils.

19. Patti was singing at the Stone Pony in Asbury Park with the Pony's regular Sunday night house band, Cats on a Smooth Surface.

20. Patti sings on David Sancious' album, *The Bridge*.

21. Patti became an official E Streeter on June 25, 1984.

22. He owns a 1948 Rock Ola jukebox.

23. Garry is credited as "Rock and Roll Historian."

24. He created the feedback in "Lost in the Flood."

25. Little Steven and the Disciples of Soul released two albums, *Men Without Women* and *Voice of America,* as of this writing.

26. He has used the nicknames Miami Steve, Sugar Steve, and Little Steven.

27. Steve receives co-producer credit on *The River* and *Born in the U.S.A.*

28. Max studied with Bernard "Pretty" Purdie.

29. *The Big Beat,* published by Contemporary Books.

30. Max played in the pit of "Godspell" and "The Magic Show."

Match-Up Quiz #6
The E Streeters

1. C
2. B
3. H
4. E
5. G
6. A
7. J
8. I
9. D
10. F
11. K

Match-Up Quiz #7
My Hometown

1. E
2. I
3. F
4. H
5. K
6. A
7. B
8. D
9. G
10. J
11. C

Match-Up Quiz #8
The Songs That Bind

1. C
2. F
3. E
4. D
5. G and H
6. A
7. B

Q and A #7
Miscellaneous

1. After a few drinks, a very loose Bruce asked DJ Mary Turner for a date while she was interviewing him. She declined.

2. The Castiles—Tex Vinyard; Earth — Rick Stachner; Child—Fran Duffy; Steel Mill—Carl "Tinker" West; The E Street Band—Mike Appel and Jon Landau.

3. Mike Appel and his partner, Jim Cretecos, worked for Wes Farrell, who handled music for The Partridge Family. Appel and Cretecos wrote a song for them that became a moderate hit, "Doesn't Somebody Want to Be Wanted."

4. Bruce told John Hammond he would never perform the song "If I Was the Priest." However, the song was recorded for the music publishing demos he made for CBS in 1972, and Allan Clarke did a cover version of it.

5. Jon Landau wrote for *The Real Paper*.

6. The fateful audition was held on the morning of May 3, 1972.

7. Bruce was officially signed five weeks later, on June 9, 1972.

8. He had read about him in a biography on Bob Dylan, another John Hammond discovery.

9. A song called "Balboa Versus the Beast Slayer."

10. Philip Elwood in the San Francisco *Examiner*.

11. He was referring to Steel Mill.

12. It appeared in *The Real Paper* on May 22, 1974.

13. They met outside Charley's in Boston on April 10, 1974.

14. It was filmed on July 8, 1978, at the Coliseum in Phoenix, Arizona.

15. On April 29, 1976, after playing the Ellis Auditorium in Memphis, Tennessee, Bruce scaled the gates of Graceland in an attempt to meet Elvis Presley. He was stopped by security guards, who told him that Elvis was in Lake Tahoe. Bruce never got to meet Elvis.

16. The magazines were issued October 27, 1975.

17. The story was called "Making of a Rock Star."

18. Kid Leo, one of Bruce's early followers, played a pre-release copy of "Born to Run."

19. Bruce appears in the USA for Africa video "We Are the World," in the "Sun City" video, and in Clarence Clemons' video, "Woman's Got the Power." To date, Bruce's own video appearances are "Rosalita," "Dancing in the Dark," "Born in the U.S.A.," "I'm on Fire," "Glory Days," "My Hometown," and "War."

20. Bruce's music appears in the movies *Ruthless People*, *Baby, It's You*, *Risky Business*, and *Wise Guys*.

21. *Risky Business* features a brief bit of "Hungry Heart." In *Ruthless People*, you hear the beginning of "Stand on It." "Pink Cadillac" was used in *Wise Guys*. But in the John Sayles' film *Baby, It's You*, you hear "It's Hard to Be a Saint in the City," "The E Street Shuffle," "She's the One," and "Adam Raised a Cain."

22. The real Cadillac Ranch is on Route 66, eight miles west of Amarillo, Texas.

23. He celebrated in a roller skating rink in Buffalo, New York.

24. The actress is Courtney Cox.

25. He was awared a Grammy for Best Male Rock Vocalist for "Dancing in the Dark."

26. The first "Dancing in the Dark" video was directed by Jeff Stein. However, Bruce was not happy with it, so he hired Brian DePalma to make another version.

27. Bruce performs "Thunder Road," "The River," and part of "Quarter to Three" in the movie *No Nukes*.

28. It said "To Be True."

29. He plays a carwash attendant.

30. Phil Petillo.

Match-Up Quiz #9
B True

1. E
2. I
3. B
4. J
5. D
6. L
7. G

8. M
9. F
10. H
11. A
12. K
13. C
14. N

Photographer John Corio and Bruce.

(photo: Debra Rothenberg)

Deborah Mayer has been in love with Springsteen's music since she was 13. A native New Yorker, Deborah lives in Manhattan and spends her summers at the Jersey Shore. She works as a television production assistant, and her credits include *The Cosby Show*, *One Life to Live*, *Gimme A Break,* and *ABC News Closeup.*

Note: Most of the photos in this book are available for purchase. For information, please contact the author, in care of Mustang Publishing, P.O. Box 9327, New Haven, CT, 06533.

More Great Books
from Mustang Publishing

The Complete Book of Beer Drinking Games by Andy Griscom, Ben Rand, & Scott Johnston. Attention party animals! With 50 of the greatest beer games in the world, this book has quickly become the beer drinkers bible. Over 90,000 sold! *"A classic in American Literature"—The Torch, St. John's Univ.* **$5.95**

Beer Games II: The Exploitative Sequel by Griscom, Rand, Johnston, & Balay. This uproarious sequel is even funnier than the original! With 30 new beer games, more hilarious articles and cartoons, and the wild Beer Catalog, this book must be seen to be believed. *"Absolutely fantastic!"—34th Street Newspaper, Univ. of Pennsylvania.* **$5.95**

Essays That Worked: 50 Essays from Successful Applications to the Nation's Top Colleges by Boykin Curry & Brian Kasbar. Applying to college? Dread the application essay? This book can help. With 50 outstanding essays from schools like Yale, Duke, and Wesleyan—plus lots of helpful advice from admissions officers—this book will challenge, amuse, and inspire any college applicant. *"Fifty essays, each one a winner"—New York Times.* **$8.95**

Mustang books should be available at your local bookstore. If not, you may order directly from us. Send a check or money order for the price of the book—plus $1.00 for postage *per book* —to Mustang Publishing, P.O. Box 9327, New Haven, CT, 06533. Please allow three weeks for delivery.